Raptors

BIRDS OF PREY

Raptors

BIRDS OF PREY

Written and Photographed by
John Hendrickson

Chronicle Books / San Francisco

Acknowledgments:

For Lincoln Vande Griendt, an ornithologist who found
the time to share knowledge and enthusiasm with a young
boy.

For Tom Rodgers, a naturalist, professor and friend, who
taught me about life, as well as birds.

For Kathe, my best friend and wife, who equally shares
and thoroughly encourages my love of birds.

And of course, for the birds themselves.

Printed in Hong Kong
Book and cover design: Gail Grant

Library of Congress Cataloging-in-Publication Data
Hendrickson, John.
    Raptors, birds of prey / written and photographed by
John Hendrickson.
    p.   cm.
    Includes index.
    ISBN 0-8118-0221-3 : $29.95
    ISBN 0-8118-0004-0 (pbk.) : $18.95
    1. Birds of prey.   I. Title.
QL696.F3H48 1992   598.9'1–dc20   92-9808
                                                 CIP

10 9 8 7 6 5 4 3 2 1

Distributed in Canada by
Raincoast Books,
112 East Third Avenue
Vancouver, B.C. V5T 1C8

Chronicle Books
275 Fifth Street
San Francisco, California 94103

Contents

Introduction

Butterflies first introduced me to birds. When I was nine, I used to pick floating butterflies out of the pond behind my house and let them dry their wings on my hands so they could fly free. Once when I was searching for butterflies, I stumbled upon a round pile of brownish fluff. When I knelt down to take a closer look, I was amazed to find a baby owl that had fallen out of its nest. I decided to climb the tree and return the lost owl to its nest, but when I reached down to pick up the bird it grabbed my hand with its sharp talons. I decided to go home and get a pair of gloves and some help.

What I got instead was poor advice. My neighbor informed me that I should not put the owl back into its nest because the mother would smell my scent and reject the baby. Not knowing any better, I brought the bird home. Since I knew nothing about raising an owl, I asked the one person in the world who knew everything: my third grade teacher. She suggested that I write a letter to a friend of hers, a young ornithology professor at the University of California named Lincoln Vande Griendt.

The friendship that followed deeply affected me. Like all good birders, Dr. Vande Griendt conveyed joy and enthusiasm that were contagious. I was amazed as he pointed out tiny specks in the

For thousands of years owls and hawks, like this western screech owl (far left) and black-shouldered kite (near left), have captured our imaginations. To ensure their futures, and the future of all raptors, we must grow from an appreciation of beauty to an understanding of ecological principles and the many challenges which raptors face.

sky and taught me how to identify turkey vultures, red-tailed hawks, and golden eagles. Dr. Vande Griendt also taught me that it is best to return a lost bird to its nest. If it's not possible to climb to the nest, the bird should be placed on the highest branch. The adults will then encourage the nestling to hop up-ward from branch to branch back into the nest. If the nestling can't make it to the nest, the adult will feed and protect the bird where it is. A returned nestling will immediately be accepted, assuming parents are still present to care for other young still in the nest. Even a chick that has been away for several days will be accepted.

Birds mature very rapidly. In three weeks my small owl had grown to full size; in another three weeks it was fully feathered and taking short flights around the yard. As suggested by Dr. Vande Griendt, I placed a small tray in the owl's favorite tree and each evening put food there. Consistently the owl returned to feed. This association, often referred to as "hacking out," continued for almost a month. Two months later, my new friend returned to the wild.

This book is an attempt to repay a lifelong debt. Birds have given me many gifts. The call of a hawk, the hoot of an owl — these are the voices of lifelong friends, friends whom I now find in trouble. With sadness, frustration, and concern I have watched raptor populations decline during the last thirty years, the vic-tims of habitat loss and chemical contamination. Many of the territories I watched for years as a child are now gone. In their place I find shopping centers, housing developments, video stores, parking lots, freeways, gas stations, and other signs of human expansion.

But there is hope. The public's opinion of raptors has changed significantly over the same thirty years. The decline of species like the peregrine falcon and bald eagle has stimulated tremendous growth in raptor research and conservation. Never before has the public been so aware of and concerned with raptors. The continued evolution of this new awareness is critical to the future health of raptors and their environment.

The most important element needed to ensure a healthy environment is an educated public. The primary intent of this book is to educate, but also to celebrate and share the beauty of raptors. If I can share my knowledge and understanding of raptors, I believe others will be encouraged to help save raptors. Then, in a small way, I will have begun to repay my debt to the birds.

Part One: Gifts of Birth

Gifts of Birth

Raptor is a relatively new term, and there is still considerable confusion as to what separates a *"raptor"* from a *"bird of prey"*. Technically, any bird that regularly feeds on other animals is a bird of prey. The great egret, for example, is a bird of prey that feeds on fish, frogs, and other aquatic animals. For most people, however, the phrase *bird of prey* conjures up images of eagles, falcons, or owls, birds with three specific anatomical features that qualify them specifically as raptors: strong grasping feet equipped with sharp talons, a hooked upper beak, and excellent binocular vision.

The thirty-three species of hawks, falcons, vultures, and eagles and the eighteen species of owls breeding in North America are the heirs apparent to forty million years of evolution. For at least that long, raptors have been flying, hunting, and struggling to survive in a slowly but constantly changing environment. Man's fascination with and admiration for raptors is also ancient, perhaps as old as man himself, for these birds are both masters of flight and supreme hunters, integrating strength, power, and beauty.

The oldest raptor fossils have all been found in North America. Many early raptors, like the huge *Teratornis incredibilis* with its

The great egret (near left) is considered a bird of prey because it regularly feeds on other animals. But the egret is not a raptor. Raptors, like the golden eagle (far left), are birds of prey that have three specialized adaptations: hooked upper beaks for tearing flesh, grasping feet equipped with talons, and excellent binocular vision.

seventeen-foot wingspan, have perished. Several large raptors are peculiar to the Pleistocene age only, most impressive among them *Harpagornis*. This enormous sea eagle of New Zealand is assumed to have preyed on giant flightless birds called moas. Moas, now also extinct, were among the largest birds ever to have lived: some stood nearly thirteen feet tall and weighed over five hundred pounds. What processes of natural selection caused early raptor species, and in some cases entire genera, to become extinct no one knows. Most likely, as the large mammals died off toward the end of the Ice Age, it became increasingly difficult for the larger raptors to find enough carcasses to supply needed food.

As with all animals, every detail of a raptor's behavior is designed to promote survival. Most birds do not begin incubation until all their eggs are laid, thus ensuring that the young will all hatch at roughly the same time. Raptors are an exception, beginning incubation when the first egg is laid. This staggered reproduction helps balance raptor populations to the available prey population; it also ensures that when food is limited a few healthy, rather than several unhealthy, birds will survive. The first hatched nestling is often considerably larger and may be over a full week older than the last hatched. This bigger and older bird is generally fed first every time. In lean times, the younger and smaller nestlings may starve while the older birds get all the available food. Sometimes the older birds even kill and eat their younger siblings.

Many raptor species, such as barn owls, lay eggs in direct relationship to the density of available prey. When rodent populations are low, barn owls breed only once a year and lay only two or three eggs. During particularly rich years, however, they are known to lay up to ten eggs in a clutch, and may breed again when the first group of young has left the nest.

To help them locate and capture prey, raptors possess some of the most specialized adaptations found in the animal kingdom: specifically adapted feet and beaks, highly developed vision and hearing, and exceptional flight capabilities. In addition, raptors are uniquely designed to quickly and efficiently process their diets. It is these gifts of birth that separate raptors from all other birds, both scientifically and in their ability to capture our fascination.

Left: Very rare in the United States, the white-tailed hawk is found only in southern Texas, where it lives in open coastal grasslands and dry brush areas.

Right: Many raptors will aggressively defend their nests. This barn owl has lowered its head and spread its wing in an attempt to appear larger in order to block its nest.

FEET

Feet are the primary weapons of death and protection for raptor species. Injured raptors on the ground almost always respond to danger by lying on their backs with feet up and open. Once raptors grab something, they generally will not let go until their catch stops moving, an innate reaction that helps keep raptors from losing their prey. Usually quite large and incredibly powerful, their feet can exert enough pressure to puncture thick skin, often crushing and killing prey instantly. The talon on the back toe is particularly long – in eagles, at least a full inch – and can be driven into its victim with impressive force. An adult golden eagle, for example, exerts approximately two hundred pounds of pressure per square inch. The feet of raptors vary in size according to their preferred prey: rodent hunters generally have short, stout toes, while bird hunters have long thin toes to increase their grasping area. The spread of a golden eagle's feet is roughly nine inches, the same as an adult man's hand with fingers outstretched.

Owls differ from most other raptors in that their feet are feathered down to the toes. (Some cold-climate hawks also have this adaptation which probably helps keep feet warm.) Another special feature of owl feet is that their outer toe is reversible: owls have two toes facing forward and two facing backward, while most other birds have three toes forward and one back. This configuration gives owls a better hold on their prey and a wider spread with their feet, an adaptation especially useful for catching prey hidden below grasses or leaves. Great horned owls kill large prey by silently approaching from behind, grasping the head with both feet, and puncturing the skull with their sharp talons.

Left: Because owls are active at night when temperatures are cooler, they have thicker feathers than diurnal raptors. Snowy owls, like the one pictured, have the thickest feathering of all birds on their legs and feet.

Right: Adult and immature bald eagles.

BEAKS

All raptors have powerful hooked upper beaks, used primarily for tearing prey rather than for killing. Bald eagles have particularly large beaks, which enable them to feed on large prey without immersing their heads in the carcass. This helps keep feathers clean and reduces the spread of bacteria. The large beaks and featherless heads of vultures serve a similar purpose. Unlike other raptors, which generally kill with their feet, falcons use their beaks both for killing and for protection. They have powerful jaw muscles, and toothlike projections that enable them to deliver a forceful bite, severing the cervical vertebrae of prey. Among raptors, this adaptation is found only in falcons.

Although their beaks are very similar, hawks and owls are not closely related. Fossil records indicate a divergence of hawks and owls into separate families at least thirty million years ago. The adaptations that they have in common are believed to be the result of convergent evolution. This theory states that when two unrelated animal groups fill similar roles in their environment, they evolve similar adaptations. The feathers which surround the beaks of owls, however, are quite different from hawks'. Owls have short, bristle-like feathers around their beaks which function like whiskers, helping owls locate prey close to their faces.

Left: Vultures have a superior olfactory sense which allows them to locate carrion. While the nostrils of other birds are separated by the nasal septum, vultures have a perforate septum. This opening in the bill may be an adaptation to enable air to flow more freely into the olfactory chambers, thus enhancing the vultures' sense of smell.

Right: Like all fish-eating eagles, the bald eagle has an extremely large beak. This adaptation enables it to feed on large fish without immersing its head in the carcass.

VISION

The best long-range vision on this planet most likely belongs to raptors as a group and eagles in particular. I once watched an adult bald eagle flying high over a ridge suddenly half-fold its wings and begin a long dive toward the distant shore of a lake. The bird never veered from its course, flying in what appeared to be a straight line for at least a mile. Reaching the lake, the eagle extended its legs and emerged from the water with a large fish. I wondered, could the eagle actually have seen that fish from such a distance?

The vision of raptors has been estimated to be at least eight times better than that of humans. What we can see at twenty feet, raptors can see at one hundred and sixty feet. This incredible eyesight is due not to telephoto or binocular eyes, which bring the image closer, but to very high resolving power. Envision a television screen made up of dots: human eyesight might resolve the image into one hundred dots; raptors would discern eight hundred.

This capacity derives from several specialized adaptations. Birds in general have extremely large eyes, often occupying a large part of the head and weighing more than the brain. The largest eyes of all land vertebrates are said to be those of the ostrich: about two inches in diameter.

If you examine the skull of any raptor, you will see that it appears to be literally built around their enormous eyes. Because the eyes have no extra room to move within their sockets, they are fixed facing forward in the head. To shift their gaze, raptors must turn their heads; they cannot roll their eyes as humans do. Raptors therefore have long, flexible necks that enable them to turn their heads and face directly backward. Most raptor species can, in fact, turn their heads two hundred and seventy degrees.

In owls, the frontal position of their eyes has important survival value. Like most animals, birds can be divided into the hunters and the hunted. The hunted have eyes on the sides of their heads, enabling all-around vision, whereas the hunters have eyes facing forward, providing overlapping vision to improve depth perception. Owls, in fact, have the most frontally situated eyes of all birds, and as a result have a visual field of only one hundred and ten degrees. (The visual field of humans, by contrast, is one hundred and eighty degrees.)

Owls also have larger eyes than do hawks and eagles. An adult great horned owl weighs only two pounds, yet its eyes are roughly the same size as human eyes. If human eyes were proportionately as large, they would be the size of softballs and weigh about five pounds each. The pupils of owls act as huge windows through which a tremendous amount of light can pass. They can be opened up very wide for night vision or, contrary to

All raptors have a third eyelid called the nictitating membrane. In addition to protecting the eye from dirt and dust, this specialized structure protects the eye from injury. This membrane can be closed, as this spotted owl is exhibiting, when a raptor is about to grab its prey, thereby saving the bird's eye from harmful scratches.

popular belief, closed to a pinpoint allowing equally excellent daylight vision. Even on the darkest night, nocturnal owls can see every tree, branch, and leaf. Their eyes have been estimated to see in dim light at least thirty-five and perhaps one hundred times better than human eyes. Research has shown that several owl species can see in the light afforded by one candle twelve hundred feet away. Imagine yourself in a completely darkened room, one-fifth of a mile long: lighting one candle anywhere in that space would enable you to see everything perfectly. Interestingly, owl pupils also act independently and can be dilated or constricted to different sizes, an adaptation unique to owls that enables each eye to adjust to a specific light intensity.

The owl retina has a large concentration of light-sensitive rods, often at the expense of color-sensitive cones. For the truly nocturnal species, this trade-off undoubtedly greatly limits their color vision. Perhaps the limited range of owl plumage hues is indicative of their inability to see color, especially at night. Where other birds use brightly colored feathers for display, owls rely more on voice and body posture.

By means of their remarkable vision owls can penetrate the darkest night, successfully weaving between trees and branches; but when it comes to finding prey, most owls depend on other sensory information. Owls are somewhat farsighted, able to focus on very near objects only with difficulty. For determining the exact location of prey they are aided by stiff feathers called rictal bristles that project outward around their beaks; these function in a way similar to cats' whiskers,

providing nonvisual information. Mice hidden by two or three inches of light snow or gently woven grasses are still vulnerable to attentively listening owls.

I once photographed a female great gray owl that was hunting along the edge of a mountain meadow near Bend, Oregon. I had been watching the bird for six hours, so it had become quite accustomed to my presence. Then, all of a sudden, the bird fully opened its eyes and began to stare intently at me, bobbing its head from side to side and up and down, a behavior used by many raptors to increase depth perception when focusing on prey. Suddenly it flew straight toward me, gliding only a foot above my head. Twenty feet beyond me it landed, reached through a light layer of snow, and promptly snatched up a vole.

Left: Red-tailed hawks use their excellent binocular vision to locate prey from exposed perches.

Right: Common Barn owl nestlings, Tyto alba.

HEARING

Hearing in the avian world is developed to the utmost in raptors. From the high-pitched call of the kestrel to the low booming notes of the great gray owl, the wide variety of noises that raptors make indicates that their hearing is both broad-ranged and acute. Most birds use hearing primarily as a means of communication, and raptors are no exception. However, raptors also use hearing as a means of locating food. Owls use hearing to locate prey they cannot see.

Owls can hear sounds that are at least ten times fainter than the human ear can detect. Large ear openings in the side of the head are surrounded by deep, soft feathers that funnel sounds to each ear. Owls are the only birds that also have a movable flap of skin, controlled by mus-

cles, around the ear openings. This specialized adaptation, it is thought, both protects the ear and helps reflect and concentrate sound waves coming from behind.

An owl's entire face functions as an outer ear. Compact facial feathers are arranged to form two parabolic curves, much like the shape of a satellite receiving disc. These tightly packed feathers help reflect and focus sounds into each ear. The same feature distinguishes the northern harrier, a hawk that often hunts by flying low over marshes, very likely using hearing to search for prey hidden beneath vegetation.

The feathers that cover the actual ear openings of owls are also specially modified. Called auriculars, they have no

Left: Northern harriers often hunt by flying low over the ground, listening, as well as looking, for prey.

Right: Once common throughout grasslands of North America, the Swainson's hawk is a victim of habitat loss and is now endangered in much of its former range.

Left: The feather tufts that many owls, such as this great horned owl, have on the top of their head have no function in hearing. Instead, they are used for display and camouflage.

Right: The heart-shaped disc of compact feathers which surrounds a barn owl's face functions as an outer ear, both reflecting and focusing sounds into the asymmetrically placed ears.

barbules (the parts of the feather that zip together making the feather wind-resistant) and so are loose and airy, allowing sounds to pass freely through. Interestingly, the feathers that many people associate with owl "ears," the tufts on such species as the great horned, long-eared, short-eared, and screech owls, have nothing to do with hearing; rather, they are used for visual display and camouflage.

Perhaps the most amazing feature of owl ears is the shape and location of the ear openings. Truly nocturnal species like the barn owl that rely most heavily on hearing to locate prey have ear openings of different shapes or placed asymmetrically on the head. By distinguishing slight variations in sound arrival time and volume, owls can precisely locate the origin of sounds on both a vertical and a horizontal plane. (When a dog cocks its head to listen more intently, it is applying the same principle.) To hear equally in both ears, an owl must slowly turn its head until it is directly facing the origin of the sound on both planes. Whether it can see its prey or not, the owl is now ready to initiate its attack.

In 1956, the scientist Roger Payne conducted a series of experiments which proved that barn owls could locate and capture prey in complete darkness. A captive-reared owl was released into a dark room with controlled artificial lighting. The floor was covered with leaves, and the owl was allowed to fly about capturing mice for several days. Then the light began progressively to be lowered in order to determine how much light the owl needed to locate and capture a mouse. To the amazement of all, even when the room was absolutely dark the owl still continued to catch mice. Thinking that the bird might be using smell or sensing infrared heat waves to locate prey, Payne dragged a small wad of paper through the leaves in complete darkness. The owl flew down and caught the paper wad. Over and over, these experiments were repeated, and in every case the owl's success rate was very high. Clearly, barn owls could locate and capture prey in total darkness using only their sense of hearing.

FLIGHT

Feathers are a bird's utmost evolutionary accomplishment: nothing can equal the combined warmth, strength, and light weight of the feather. And yet, a bird's skeleton usually weighs less than the combined weight of the feathers, while remaining remarkably strong. Flying machines need to be light but rigid, so in the avian skeleton many of the smaller bones found in mammals or reptiles have been fused or eliminated. Teeth, for example, and the heavy jaws to hold them, are gone. Instead, birds use muscular gizzards and strong digestive systems to "chew" their food internally, between the wings, where they can carry weight. Then, too, most birds have bones that contain air, rather than marrow. Indeed, the longer limb bones can be almost completely hollow, having only an internal system of struts for support. The inner air provides good shock absorption, and hollow bones bend more easily than solid bones, thus providing more strength.

To help supply the large amounts of oxygen necessary for flight, a series of air sacs supplement a bird's lungs, enabling the bird to inhale more air than its lungs can hold. The air sacs fill available space in the body and, in soaring species, extend into the large hollow bones. This extra air not only contributes to a respiratory system that is the most efficient of all vertebrates, but it also serves to ventilate or cool the bird's interior.

Raptors have various adaptations that assist them in flight. A flying owl, for instance, while approaching hidden prey, must intently listen for and adjust to prey movements. The stiff noisy feathers of most birds would interfere with a successful hunt. Most owls, therefore, have soft, flexible feathers – and thus nearly silent flight, giving them the advantage of surprise. The first primary of an owl's wing (its leading feather) has a uniquely toothed or serrated front edge, which is also found to a lesser degree on the second and third primaries. These comblike edgings help break up the flow of air and deaden the sound of wind rushing across the wing. In addition, owls have large broad wings, which enable slow, gliding flight.

Unlike owls, hawks must see their prey in order to catch it, and so they must hunt over a larger area. Many species have adapted to hunting on the wing, with the long, broad wings and tails of eagles, vultures, and hawks from the genus *Buteo* facilitating nearly effortless flight. These birds must fly for hours searching the ground for food without exhausting themselves. Thus, rather than flapping, they travel by riding thermals, gliding from one column of rising hot air to the next. Individual primary feathers are separated at the wingtips to provide air slots and act as miniature winglets, each feather providing additional lift and fine adjustment.

Without question, the most incredible and important adaptation of all birds is the feather. Whether feathers first evolved to keep birds warm, dry, cool, or to help them fly, they now perform all these functions. When hunting, most raptors, like the osprey at right, keep their feet open so the sharp talons will be poised to capture prey.

In contrast to the slow soaring flight of vultures, eagles, and buteos, hawks of the genus *Accipiter* have short, rounded wings and long tails, providing quick acceleration and maneuverability. I once watched a sharp-shinned hawk catch a barn swallow in midair, having pursued its quarry for over a hundred yards. Each twist, turn, and dodge of the swallow was duplicated with amazing precision by the agile hawk.

Still another pattern is exemplified by the falcon. Rather than effortlessly soar and then drop on their prey, or pursue prey in a tail chase of agility, large falcons use intense speed to deliver bone-breaking midair blows to kill prey. Indeed, falcons are without question the fastest animals on earth. Estimates of a diving peregrine's speed range from one hundred to two hundred and thirty miles per hour, and they may well fly even faster. A peregrine's compact feathers, long, narrow pointed wings with stiff quills, short necks, strong shoulders, and large pectoral muscles are all specially adapted for speed. Even the nostrils (nares) of falcons include a bony structure that forms a whorled, conchlike air passage and may help to break up the rush of incoming air. At speeds of some two hundred miles per hour, the thrust of unchecked air would make breathing difficult and could even damage the bird's lungs. Nevertheless, the exact function of the bony structures remains a mystery.

Once while camping near a peregrine's nest in the Northwest Territories of Canada, I observed a bald eagle fly through the peregrine's territory. The enraged falcon flew out from her cliffside nest and quickly placed herself about five hundred feet directly above the eagle.

Tucking her wings in tightly to her body, the falcon then went into a characteristic dive, or "stoop." Hearing the screaming falcon approach, the eagle rolled over in flight and defensively presented itself feet up. The falcon came within a foot of the eagle before it spread its wings and shot back up. They repeated this scenario at least ten times, and on each occasion the eagle lost altitude as it rolled over to defend itself. Finally the retreating eagle was driven into thick forest, where I heard it crash into the brush. Satisfied that the danger was removed, the falcon returned to her nest. Although much more powerful on the ground, an eagle in the air is no match for a falcon's speed.

On another occasion, I observed an excellent falconer working with a well-trained peregrine. The falcon had been taught to "wait on" – that is, to circle directly overhead while the falconer and his dog tried to locate and flush game. The bird went way up, almost out of sight. Then waving arms and a shout from the falconer flushed five pigeons, one pigeon of which was missing a few feathers and flew slightly behind the others. Dropping faster than a stone, the peregrine accelerated into a long stoop; it appeared to jerk through the air, an illusion created by the intense speed. On this day the peregrine was lucky: the falcon struck the slow pigeon on the first stoop. The pigeon appeared to be instantly killed, falling lifelessly from the sky. Much to my amaze- ment, however, the show was not over. The falcon flew a short distance away, turned, and, flying with its back towards the ground, caught the falling pigeon.

Large falcons, like this gryfalcon, are perhaps the ultimate flying machines; every detail of their anatomy is designed for speed.

DIET

Birds must keep their weight down so they can fly; they therefore have a specialized digestive system that gets food rapidly into the bloodstream. Further, because raptors, like most predators, never know when their next meal will be, they must be well adapted to feast and famine. In their esophagus is an enlarged area called the crop, providing additional space for the ingestion of large amounts of food. A large, well-fed raptor with a crop full of food can usually survive for at least five to seven days without eating.

Raptors often swallow their prey whole. Rather than waste digestive energy on feathers and fur, the bird somehow refashions these and other nonnutritive objects into a pellet and coughs it up, usually within twenty-four hours after eating. Amazingly, when the pellet comes up, the bones are always wrapped inside the fur or feathers. This behavior is not only efficient, but it also appears to be necessary to good health.

Pellets, often found below frequently used roosts, tell much about the raptor from which they came. If the pellet contains very few bones and is full of feathers or fur, it probably comes from a hawk, which is able to partly digest bones, rather than an owl, which is not. Owl pellets, it follows, are full of bones, analysis of which will indicate the raptor's diet, with continued collection throughout the year of sufficient pellets giving an accurate view of the raptor's overall feeding habits.

A young boy once informed me that an owl was living in his barn and eating the family's chickens. His father was going to shoot the owl. Hoping to save the bird and educate the boy, I offered to trap and

remove the owl as an alternative to shooting it. When I arrived at the barn I looked up to see a roosting barn owl. I tried to explain that barn owls hunt small rodents and that a one-pound owl could not possibly kill a five-pound chicken. Somewhat frustrated that my words were having little effect, I bent down and picked up several pellets. Neither the father nor the son had any idea what the pellets were. We opened up and examined about ten pellets and found nothing but rodent bones and fur. The boy's father, convinced that the owl was not eating his chickens, now insisted that the owl should remain.

Later that year, the same farmer called to say that his son had found a sick turkey vulture. The bird had gotten itself

Left: While most birds do not have an acute sense of smell, the great horned owl's sense is probably nonexistent; this is the only bird that regularly preys on skunks despite their strong odor.

Right: An owl pellet composed of rodent bones and fur.

entangled in a fence, and when the boy approached, the bird vomited several times. After listening to the story, I explained that the bird was probably fine. Vultures on the ground are very vulnerable to predators. Their takeoff is slow, and once cornered, a vulture is not prepared to stand and fight. Its weak feet are adapted for walking and are of little use for defense. As a result, vultures exhibit some unique behaviors of self-protection. When provoked, for example, they regurgitate their last meal: the putrid smell of partially digested carrion, surely, would be enough to repel almost any predator.

The food preferences and digestive system of vultures are truly amazing. How anything can live on a diet of rotting and often diseased carrion is a wonder, and a service to us all. Vultures lack the sharp talons of other raptors, and so, rather than killing their own prey, they live entirely on carrion. By quickly disposing of infected carcasses, vultures help to reduce the spread of diseases. A highly acid digestive system kills many viruses and some of the most virulent strains of bacteria. Some unique external adaptations also work to destroy bacteria. Vultures' bare, featherless heads are well adapted for reaching into large carcasses and staying clean. Hot, dry skin, exposed to the ultraviolet rays of the sun, does not encourage bacterial growth like wet matted feathers would. Vultures also have an interesting habit of defecating onto their own legs; again, the high acidity of their feces probably has a sterilizing function.

Part Two: The Struggle to Survive

The Struggle to Survive

By common misconception, the life of a hawk, owl, or eagle is easy. In fact, natural pressures like disease, poor weather, predation, and, above all, the struggle to find food make survival difficult. Despite forty million years of natural selection and a long list of adaptations, the odds of survival are clearly against young raptors striving to become adults.

Many people mistakenly think that raptors have few, if any, natural enemies, but in fact many creatures attack raptors. The pressures of survival begin immediately, for eggs are a favorite meal of raccoons, crows, and other predators. Ground nesters, like the northern harrier and short-eared owl, are particularly vulnerable. Human disturbances also increase the odds of egg predation. Most raptors can easily defend their nest against a crow, but when the presence of humans causes a raptor to leave its nest, crows, less intimidated by humans, quickly move in finding a ready-made feast. The odds of predation only increase once the eggs hatch.

Once we understand how difficult it is for raptors to survive naturally, we can begin to appreciate the significance of added human-caused threats to their survival.

DEFENSIVE BEHAVIOR

Most raptors protect their young, but the degree of protectiveness is highly variable. While many species will attack a predator ferociously, others do absolutely nothing. Golden eagles, for example, fly away at any threat, presumably confident that their young can defend themselves. My first encounter with nesting golden eagles occurred when I accompanied a biologist who was banding the young. We hiked straight up a very steep ridge for about a mile and a half, then stopped in a small clearing where we could observe a large nest approximately three hundred yards away. The female, noticing us immediately, left her nest and flew straight toward us. I was at first excited with the spectacular view, but as she continued her direct approach my excitement turned to appre-

hension. When she was just twenty feet away we hit the dirt; the eagle passed right overhead. She then flew half a mile off, where she watched us climb to the nest and band her young.

Falcons, in contrast, usually defend their nests quite aggressively. Small kestrels stoop and dive at the heads of intruders, and larger falcons, like peregrines, may use their feet and intense speed to deliver severe blows to the head. Most attacks involve no direct contact but only high-speed passes that come within inches of the target; yet there are always exceptions. On one occasion when I was setting up a blind, a pair of prairie falcons worked as a team to drive me away from their nesting territory. The two birds flew in tight formation, the male about ten feet in front of the female. Moreover, they attacked straight down the line of the sun, so that when I looked up to see my assailants I was looking into the sun. The male seemed to be flying interference, for he never actually struck me. But the female, following just a half a second behind her mate, hit me every time with closed feet. Each powerful blow felt like I was being hit with a fast-pitch baseball.

Many owl species exhibit threatening behavior that does not involve physical contact or violence. They fluff their feathers and flip their wings inside out, fanning them out around the body; they then crouch down and loudly snap their beaks open and closed. This fierce pose makes the birds appear to double in size. Although I have witnessed this defensive posture several times, I have never actually been attacked by an owl. However, accounts of serious injury resulting from owl attacks are on record.

Left: Exhibiting a behavior known as mobbing, an aggressive Steller's jay tries to force a roosting great horned owl from its perch.

Right: The young screech owl on the top branch is there for a reason. It is the first-born, the dominate sibling. This bird is larger and healthier because it is fed first every time.

The longer a bird must stay in the nest, the lower its chances of survival. Wind, severe storms, and predation all limit fledgling success. Even once they leave the nest, of course, the threat of predation remains. Larger raptors frequently prey on smaller raptor species. The remains of red-tailed hawks and great horned owls, for instance, have been found in the nests of golden eagles. I once saw a prairie falcon kill a burrowing owl. Peregrines are known to kill kestrels, and great horned owls kill many smaller raptors, both diurnal and nocturnal. Large owls, especially great horned owls, will prey at night on the nestlings of many diurnal raptor species, including eagles. During the day, eagles and large hawks turn the tables and often prey on nestling owls. This constant predatory pressure has led to the development of some interesting protective behaviors and adaptations.

For several weeks during the breeding season, small woodland owls like the saw-whet call loudly to advertise territory and attract a mate, making it impossible to locate and observe them at close range. One evening, quite by accident, I discovered one of the saw-whet owl's protective adaptations. After a long, quiet approach, I was certain that the still calling owl was directly in front of me, not more than thirty feet away. When I turned on my flashlight, however, the small owl flew not from the spot where I expected it to be, but from a spot at least twenty feet away, forty-five degrees to my left. I have since observed this behavior several times and realized that saw-whet owls have the unique ability to throw their voices – effective concealment from nearby larger owls that might otherwise turn the calling saw-whet into an easy meal.

Top Right: Prairie falcon.

Bottom Right: Northern saw-whet owl.

Left: Long before they can fly, young raptors leave the nest and begin to wander to nearby branches or vegetation. Called branchers, most spread out with the intention that an arriving predator will not find and kill the entire brood. In addition, as young birds grow, many nests become overcrowded. By spreading out, young are less likely to fall.

CAMOUFLAGE

The immature plumage of most raptors is beautifully camouflaged to match the colors and patterns of their environment, later giving way, in all but the owls, to a brighter, more colorful breeding plumage. Because owls have very limited color vision and use voice to attract a mate, their plumage is especially camouflaged. Even the most cryptically colored animal, however, is easy to see if it moves. Roosting owls sit very still and are often quite hesitant to fly. They further their concealment by perching next to the trunks of trees or hiding in dense foliage. Several species use old woodpecker nests, tree cavities, or even caves as daytime roosts. When disturbed, many species raise their ear tufts, compress their feathers, and stand erect. This behavior helps narrow an owl's silhouette, causing it to look like an old stump or broken branch. When searching for owls I rarely look up; I look down. The odds of spotting a perfectly still, highly camouflaged owl are slim. So rather than search the trees, I search the ground for pellets and white droppings. Occasionally, upon finding fresh droppings, I have looked up to see the intent eyes of a roosting owl. At other times, though, even when I was certain an owl was present, I have been unable to spot it.

Roosting owls often seem unconcerned with the presence of humans, preferring to

sit still rather than fly, thus affording easy, prolonged observation. I once found a spotted owl roosting about twenty feet up a large fir. I walked all around the tree, but could not get a clear view. The bird seemed very relaxed, so I decided to climb a nearby tree in the hopes of gaining an unobstructed view. The owl calmly watched as I climbed, equipment dangling, to its eye level, took thirty photographs, climbed down, and left.

The camouflaged coloration of owls certainly helps them hide from potential predators, but perhaps more importantly, it also enables them to sleep peacefully during the day. For in order to rest, an owl must hide. Many small birds, upon recognizing the shape of an owl (or to a lesser

Neither nocturnal nor diurnal, the great horned owl is considered to be a crepuscular species, meaning that it is active primarily at dusk and dawn.

degree, a hawk), instinctively react with an attacking behavior called mobbing. The strategy here generally involves making as much noise as possible, with crows, jays, robins, chickadees, kinglets, titmice, bush-tits, sparrows, blackbirds, and humming-birds being the most aggressive mobbers. Loud scolding calls advertise the predator's presence and attract other birds to the battle. Soon the mobbing behavior and scolding of one bird will have generated a small army. Interestingly, it is not only birds of the same species that respond, but other species join in as well, seemingly cooperating toward a common goal. Although usually unsuccessful, the birds are intent on driving the owl away, espe-cially in the hours before nightfall. Once while searching for nesting owls I ob-

served some thirty birds enthusiastically mobbing one small pygmy owl – a notori-ous predator of other birds. Curiously, the coloration of pygmy owls creates the impression of two open eyes on the back of their heads. Although current literature states that this adaptation discourages attacks by larger predators, this is some-what doubtful, since most predators of pygmy owls probably do not care whether the owl is looking or not. Songbirds, how-ever, likely are intimidated by an alert gaze. For that reason, and because song-birds generally attack owls from the rear, I believe the pygmy owl's false eye spots function primarily to deter mobbing birds.

Far Left: Rough-legged hawk on burnt snag.

Near Left: Pygmy owl with a captured wren.

Opposite: Freezing in its tracks, this long-eared owl attempts to blend in with the tree branch.

Young raptors that are lucky enough to avoid predation, both as nestlings and as young fledglings, still must face an even bigger potential killer: winter. Studies consistently indicate that over fifty percent of all the raptors that successfully leave the nest die during their first year, the majority in winter. The highest death rates of adults, too, occur in winter.

Competition for limited food is constant and especially intense in winter. A raptor that has successfully located and captured prey may well be deprived of the opportunity to eat its rightful meal. Predatory mammals, larger raptors, and individuals of the same species are quick to pirate food from a successful hunter. Battles can involve several species and last for hours.

To observe this intense competition for winter food, I traveled to the northeastern corner of California, where large concentrations of wintering bald eagles gather. On my way to the blind I collected dead ducks and geese, which I placed ten to seventy feet from my watching post. For five days, only magpies and crows were drawn to the bait. Either food was abundant or else wary raptors preferred to watch and let other birds test the safety of the situation. On the sixth day, a male northern harrier hawk came to feed on a duck carcass. An immature female arrived next and, rather than take one of the unclaimed carcasses, drove the male away. The displaced male flew to another nearby carcass and continued feeding. As more harriers arrived, each new bird forcibly took over occupied carcasses rather than settling for available food. Red-tailed hawks and rough-legged hawks repeated

Right: Although all raptors, like these northern harriers, have powerful feet equipped with sharp talons, they rarely use them against each other when fighting over scarce prey.

Opposite: Severe winter storms often ground soaring birds, like this golden eagle, making hunting very difficult.

the competitive behavior of the harriers. The jockeying for food was so intense that the birds seemed to spend more time flying and fighting than eating. Ten to fifteen different species might partake of a single duck before it was consumed.

Later that same day, an adult golden eagle arrived to join in the feast. Without landing, the eagle grabbed a goose carcass and carried it less than ten feet away from my blind. The eagle was so close that I could hear it tearing into the flesh of the goose. Abruptly the eagle stood erect, raised its golden head feathers, and spread its wings and tail in an attempt to hide the goose carcass, a common behavior to most raptors called mantling. I now saw that an adult bald eagle had landed about twenty feet away from the golden eagle and was beginning slowly to approach the golden's food. Suddenly, the two birds flew at each other, rose into the air, and met feet to feet in combat. The battle lasted only seconds before the golden eagle returned to its meal and the bald eagle flew away.

For most raptors, winter is the season of stress, starvation, and death. Cold temperatures require birds to use more energy, increasing food intake in an effort to stay warm. At the same time, inclement weather and shortened daylight make finding food more difficult. •

Top: This golden eagle did not kill the deer, it is feeding on carrion, a common practice which often erroneously gives eagles the reputation of killing livestock.

Bottom: In this sequence, a golden eagle begins to feed on a rabbit, but when another eagle flies overhead the feeding eagle spreads its wings and tail in an attempt to hide its prey. This mantling behavior is common to all raptors.

45

MIGRATION

Freezes or droughts that limit the growth of plants in turn create food shortages for rodents. As rodent populations decrease, a potential food source for raptors also decreases. At the same time, cold winter temperatures increase a raptor's food requirements, while short days and inclement weather make finding prey even more difficult. Weakened birds are more susceptible to disease. Desperate and starving young birds take more chances, approaching human settlements in search of food. Birds must adapt to the stresses of winter by either changing their behavior or changing their location, or both.

Some raptor species change location with spectacular migrations. The most notable migrators are the broad-winged hawk, Swainson's hawk, osprey, and tundra peregrine falcon. Broad-wings tend to form large groups and fly along established routes. Throughout the United States, especially in the east, you can go to any of nearly two hundred different hawk migration lookouts to watch these impressive flights. If you are lucky enough to hit the right spot at the right time, you might see more than ten thousand migrating birds. On one spectacular day in 1961, observers at Hawk Cliffs, a lookout on the shore of Lake Erie, counted more than seventy thousand broad-wings migrating from their Canadian nesting territories south toward wintering grounds in Central America.

Some luck is always involved because the exact date of the migration peak varies from year to year. Fall movements are generally associated in the east with northeast winds and a rising barometer, weather phenomena that often follow storms. Diurnal raptors usually do not migrate in the rain, and they never migrate at night. Little is known about owl migration except that most owls – the flammulated owl and, to a lesser degree, the elf owl being the exceptions – migrate only sporadically and do not adhere to a true migration pattern.

The migrations of soaring raptors are powered by solar energy. As the sun warms open areas, bubbles of hot air, or "thermals," begin to rise because hot air is lighter than cold air. Raptors quickly locate the best thermals and place themselves directly in the currents of rising hot air. When one bird is rising quickly, others will leave their thermals for the more favored spot. The gradual concentration of birds into one preferred thermal can create a spectacular sight as hundreds, and sometimes thousands, of birds circle and swirl in crisscrossing spirals – formations that are aptly called boils or kettles. If a thermal is particularly large, raptors may climb up to three miles above the ground before setting their wings for the long downward glide to the next thermal. In this way, under ideal conditions raptors can cover

Thermals are formed when the sun warms the air along the ground, and the hot air rises. Raptors then place themselves in the middle of the rising air and effortlessly float upward until they can drift downward toward another thermal. In this way, birds are capable of flying great distances while exerting little energy.

great distances with little energy output. Very few species, it should be noted, stay in their nesting territories year-round. For instance, bald eagles that breed in California and Florida go north to Canada and Alaska in late summer. Many prairie falcons and ferruginous hawks follow an east-west movement to winter on the Great Plains. Typically, birds breeding in the mountains, such as red-tailed hawks, drop down in elevation during the winter to concentrate in agricultural valleys where rains often flood fields, making rodents readily available. Several northern species migrate south only occasionally in loosely structured cycles. In all cases, the primary factor that forces movement is dwindling food supplies.

The coniferous trees of the northern boreal forest have a cyclic rhythm of cone production. About every third or fourth year production is high and, as a result, rodents feed and reproduce well. Not surprisingly, raptor populations that feed on these mice, voles, and squirrels also increase. During the year after high cone production, however, trees often enter a resting period and produce very few cones. Rodents starve, forcing raptor populations either to move or to starve as well. The northern species that are most affected by this cycle are the snowy owl, short-eared owl, and the rough-legged hawk. Massive southward invasions of these species occur therefore every three to four years, when cone production is low in

Rodents and insects make up the bulk of a raptor's diet. Hungry birds, however, like this great gray owl (left) and red-tailed hawk (right), often feed on unusual prey to avoid starvation.

Opposite: A bird of arctic tundra and rocky outcrops, gryfalcons are rare throughout their range. Although they are generally non-migratory, gryfalcons occasionally move southward when populations of their primary prey, ptarmigan, decline.

their northern forest homes. Northern goshawks and great horned owls feed primarily on grouse and snowshoe hares, populations that experience significant declines on a regular basis, every eight to ten years. When this occurs, these raptors migrate south in large numbers. Gyrfalcons and their prey, ptarmigans, follow a similar eight-to-ten year cycle.

Movements of great gray owls and boreal owls often occur in February. At this time of year, the weather pattern is one of warm days followed by cold nights: snow melts during the day and freezes at night, forming a crust of ice. If the weather then turns and stays cold, these crusts form an impenetrable shield of ice that protects the rodents below. This situation is most likely what forces the owls' to move southward. Predation, disease, starvation, migration,

and winter all take their toll on both the young and the old. If a bird can survive its first year, however, the hunting knowledge and skills it gains may enable it to live for a surprisingly long time. It is difficult to determine how long raptors live in the wild, for to do so requires that they be captured, banded, released, and then recovered after death. Yet although good records are scarce, those that exist are impressive: golden eagle, twenty-five years; peregrine falcon, fourteen years; red-tailed hawk, sixteen years. Captive raptors, protected from the stresses of starvation, predation, and weather, live longer still. One captive golden eagle lived forty-six years, a peregrine lived eighteen years, and a red-tailed hawk lived twenty-one years.

Left: Found throughout the world, the peregrine falcon has a range more extensive than any other bird's.

Right: Adult and immature bald eagles. Bald eagles do not acquire the characteristic white head and tail until they are three to four years old.

Part Three: Living in Balance

Living in Balance

More than forty years ago, ecological studies proved that the relationship between predator and prey is complementary. Like all predators, raptors help to stabilize their prey populations by feeding primarily on abundant species and, more specifically, on animals that have become vulnerable owing to such factors as overpopulation, disease, injury, and age. Predation, in short, helps to eliminate the peaks of overpopulation as well as the ravages of starvation and disease that would otherwise follow. If prey populations decline, raptors must switch to an alternate species, move to a new location, or die.

For years, however, hunters mistakenly blamed raptors for declines in game species. Many, for instance, believed that peregrines (then called duck hawks) killed several ducks a day, and considered competitors, hundreds were shot. Actually, one duck will feed a falcon for several days. Raptors, moreover, will not kill without hunger because of the risk of injury.

Through evolution, raptors have become better and better at finding and capturing prey. At the same time, the prey have also evolved, becoming ever more difficult to locate and catch. This process is known as

All raptors, like this broad-winged hawk, play an integral role in maintaining the balance between life, death, and renewal. From the deadest branch, to the mushrooms that rodents feed on, to the raptors that prey upon the rodents, everything is interwoven into the strands of the raptor's environment.

coevolution. Predators thus concentrate on prey that are relatively easy to capture; and to avoid elimination, the prey try to stay one step ahead of the predator: "survival of the fittest" at work.

A few raptor species have become specialists, hunting and preying on only one or a very few species. When their prey are numerous, hunting efficiency is high and populations of these specialists increase. When prey populations decrease, however, specialists that are unable to switch to another food source may become rare or even extinct. The snail kite, formerly called the Everglade kite, is perhaps the most specialized raptor in North America: its bill is specifically adapted to eat large apple snails. Unfortunately, the habitat the kites and snails occupy in southern Florida has been severely altered by irrigation and other manipulations of water levels, causing a drastic decrease in the snail population. Because the kites cannot readily eat other types of prey, they are in danger of becoming extinct in Florida.

Specialists are the exception, however, for most raptors eat several types of prey. As a rule, the more complicated and diverse the food web is, the more stable is the ecosystem. Simple food chains, like that of the apple snail and snail kite, are very vulnerable to change because there are few components to adapt to new circumstances. The importance of diversity to ecological stability cannot be overemphasized: each and every organism is in some way connected to all others and important to the stability of the whole.

Despite the high percentage of raptors that die during their first year, overall raptor populations have remained relative-

Left: Screech owl during spring storm.

Right: The tiny elf owl stands only five inches tall and weighs just three ounces, making it the smallest owl in the world.

ly stable for thousands of years – until, that is, late in the nineteenth century. Annual fluctuations up and down occurred, but prior to human disturbance the net birth and survival rate roughly equaled the death rate. Like anything in balance, however, this equation is subject to upset by even the slightest change. Natural factors generally threaten only the survival of individual birds, with population change reflecting overall population density. When numbers increase, for example, the death rate for first-year birds also climbs. Human activities, however, can negatively affect wildlife groups regardless of age or overall population density, threatening not only individual birds but entire species.

HABITAT DESTRUCTION

I had the good fortune to grow up in a home surrounded by open space and thick woodlands. My friends and I spent hours exploring nearby creeks, canyons, and hills. We knew where the raccoon den was, where the fox and opossum lived, where snakes, turtles, frogs, and lizards could be found, and where the great horned owl nested. Now when I return to this area I walk the same hills with my children, but we can't follow the old trails. Houses, streets, shopping centers, and other expressions of a constantly growing human population have transformed what was once open land. The city, once twenty miles away, seems much closer now.

As a boy, I walked about half a mile each morning to catch the school bus and then rode ten miles to school. It was from the bus window that I spotted my first red-tailed hawk nest, about one hundred and fifty yards from the main road but with miles of open space beyond. For three years during spring months I sat on the right-hand side of the bus where I could see the nesting hawks each morning.

During the fourth year, a real estate corporation purchased all the ranch land that surrounded the hawk's nest. Seventy homes, tennis courts, a swimming pool, and new roads were constructed. The red-tails moved to the other side of the road, where a small pocket of trees still remained. A year later the road was widened into a freeway, forcing the red-tails to move again. They established new nesting territory two miles away on an open hillside above town. The following year that hill was bulldozed and removed to accommodate a new rapid transit system. I never saw the birds again.

People usually notice massive and abrupt changes in their environment and recognize that many of these changes will negatively affect wildlife. Minor changes, though, often go unnoticed. One man cuts just a few trees to build a house, another cuts a little firewood each winter, and perhaps a third clears some woodland for crop planting. To the untrained eye such changes appear to be insignificant since other wildlife is still present in the area; if need be, people believe, the disturbed animals will simply move to a new area. But that is rarely possible. In a world of shrinking open space, very few vacant territories remain for uprooted wildlife.

Imbalance tips the scale in both directions. As human populations increase, wildlife populations decline. Few raptors

Although this red-tailed hawk looks like an albino, it actually has several dark spots on its body and its tail feathers are red. Pure albinos are extremely rare, less than one percent of the population.

Look closely at these two photographs. The Cooper's hawk in the top photo built this nest and raised three young. The following year, long-eared owls, who never build their own nests, claimed it to raise their young.

are well adapted to nest and find food in cities, housing developments, and shopping centers. The draining and filling of wetlands, conversion of grasslands and riparian woodlands to agriculture, and cutting of forests, not to mention less obvious activities such as the agricultural use of chemicals, have all taken their toll. During the last century, raptor populations have declined worldwide.

A raptor requires many things from its environment: nesting sites, hunting perches, sheltered roosts, food, and most important, territory. Territory is where an individual raptor hunts or nests, and others of the same species are driven out. Territory is essential to reduce the otherwise constant competition for these limited resources.

The specific area where an animal lives and can find essential life-giving resources is called its habitat. Many people think of habitat as simply an animal's home or the place where it lives. Habitat is actually much more: it must provide an animal with clean food and water, breathable air, shelter, and territory for breeding, nesting, and hunting. In almost all habitats, some resource exists in shorter supply than the others. There may, for example, be plenty of food, water, and shelter but very few trees suitable for nesting. The resource in short supply will function as a limiting factor, holding population numbers down to a level that can be supported by that resource. The total number of individuals that a particular environment can maintain in a healthy condition over a relatively long period of time is called its carrying capacity. The loss or reduction of any habitat component will act as a limiting

factor and lower that habitat's carrying capacity.

In most areas of the world, tremendous reductions in available habitat mean that few, if any, unoccupied territories remain. Adult birds fiercely defend their established winter and breeding territories and return to precisely the same areas year after year, despite distances of hundreds of miles. When an adult bird dies, its newly opened territory is usually quickly located and occupied by a young raptor of the same species. Young birds that are unable to locate quality habitat and establish hunting territory will likely die during their first winter.

The continuing growth of human populations and resultant habitat alteration and

destruction is the most serious long-term threat to wildlife. Throughout the world, most raptors are listed as endangered, threatened, or species of special concern in at least part of their range. Conserving these reduced populations and habitats is a complex challenge of political and economic import.

Like most raptors, spotted owls are intricately woven into the fabric of their habitat, being specifically adapted to live and take prey in old-growth forest ecosystems. These uncut and little-touched virgin timberlands, containing stands of huge trees, many over six hundred years old, are characterized by thick overstory vegetation and varied canopy levels, creating a cool microclimate that spotted owls depend on for survival. They also provide habitat for the owl's primary prey species,

flying squirrels and other tree-dwelling rodents. Another characteristic of old-growth is the presence of large dead trees, snags used by spotted owls for nesting. Lastly, and quite importantly, old growth provides protection from great horned owls, which generally do not hunt in thick forests. If any of these habitat components are removed, the owl's odds of survival drop significantly. And in fact, over ninety percent of the United States' original old-growth forests have already been cut, with current harvest rates estimated at more than one square mile per week. Further destruction of old-growth, experts insist, may well cause the extinction of the spotted owl.

Goshawks also nest in the large trees of old-growth forests. Where vast forests once enabled these two species to stay

The complex struggle to maintain adequate wildlife habitat is perhaps best illustrated by the spotted owl's need for old-growth forests. Each nesting pair requires approximately one thousand acres of ancient forest to live; that same area contains as much as sixteen million dollars worth of timber. The future of the spotted owl lies in the protection of its valuable habitat.

apart, the cutting of timber has now forced them uncomfortably to share pockets of remaining habitat. This unnatural situation undoubtedly increases spotted owl nestling mortality: small, fluffy owlets are easy prey for a hunting goshawk. Spotted owls have recently been found nesting in second-growth forest, but it is not yet known to what degree the young from these nests successfully fledge and mature. My own observations indicate extremely high nestling mortality at second-growth nesting sites, where great horned owls can hunt easily.

The presence of spotted owls in second-growth forests and other unnatural locations, such as agricultural valleys and urban areas, is not an indication that these owls can adapt and survive in a wide variety of habitats. Rather, it indicates a species in trouble. Birds unable to find unoccupied old-growth habitat try to survive in whatever is left, but ultimately they die. Current research indicates a ninety-five percent death rate of first-year spotted owls who attempt to live in areas that do not contain old-growth.

The struggle to save the spotted owl's habitat is only one example from a long list of endangered habitats. Swainson's hawks in California, which once nested in the vast grasslands of the Central Valley, now find only fields of agricultural cropland. They are listed as an endangered species. Goshawks in Germany have gone the way of the German forests. California condors, also an endangered species, will not survive without habitat, even if breeding is successful. Habitat destruction has caused a greater reduction in raptor and other wildlife populations worldwide than any other single factor. It seems imperative that we take heed and attempt to set things aright now, before more species are lost.

CHEMICAL CONTAMINATION

Left: The national bird of Mexico, the crested caracara is also found in Florida, Texas, and Arizona. This raptor is declining throughout its range primarily because of loss of habitat.

Right: While most raptors received federal protection in the early 1950s, the sharp-shinned hawk was one of the last birds to receive this important protection in 1972.

Despite historical carnage, most raptor populations were able to recover and stabilize to the degree that habitat existed. Then during the 1950s and 1960s, populations of several species declined drastically, even in what appeared to be quality habitat. After extensive research, the primary culprit was finally identified as pesticides, particularly DDT.

The discovery of DDT in Switzerland in 1939 ushered in a new era of pesticides. It was considered to be a miracle eradicant, cheap and effective, and it virtually eliminated many diseases spread by insects. The man who discovered the compound, in fact, received the Nobel Prize for medicine. Unfortunately, it was not extensively tested before gaining widespread use.

DDT belongs to the group of chemical compounds known as organochlorines, which also includes cyclodienes such as dieldrin, endrin, aldrin, and heptachlor. In addition to being toxic, all of these compounds are particularly harmful to wildlife for three primary reasons. First, they are chemically very stable and remain in the environment relatively unchanged for many years. Second, because these compounds dissolve in fats, they accumulate and remain in the animals that consume the poison. Thus, they readily pass from prey to predator. And third, organochlorines are dispersed over wide geographic areas by wind, water, and in the bodies of migratory animals. Researchers were initially surprised to find that even arctic peregrines, who live far from any agricultural areas, had high levels of DDT in their tissues.

By the time toxic chemicals have worked their way through the food chain and become incorporated in the tissues of a raptor, they may be several million times more concentrated than when they are first applied to the environment. Studies consistently indicate that when different organisms from the same location are examined, pesticide concentrations are lowest in plants, higher in herbivores, and highest in carnivores. Aquatic ecosystems tend to concentrate pollutants more quickly than terrestrial systems, probably because fish and many other aquatic animals absorb pesticides not only from their food, but also directly from the water through their gills. Raptors that feed on fish have much higher pesticide levels than other raptors that feed only on herbivorous mammals. In one typical study, the eggs

of rodent-eating golden eagles were found to contain pesticide concentrations of two parts per million; the concentrations in the eggs of bird-eating peregrine falcons, in contrast, registered at twenty-three parts per million.

Once ingested and absorbed into a raptor's body, DDT is changed into a more stable metabolite, DDE. This compound slows or prevents the deposition of calcium into eggshells. As a result, birds lay very thin shells that crack or dehydrate before hatching. By 1964, twenty-five years after the development of DDT, the average shell weight of peregrine falcons had decreased by thirty-two percent. In all the years of recorded research, no precedent could be found for this drastic eggshell thinning.

Because of its hazards, the United States banned DDT in 1972, and dieldrin in 1974. Many species, however, continue even today to show high levels of DDE in their eggs, even when local prey is apparently uncontaminated. A cracked bald eagle egg collected in California in 1986, for example, contained the highest levels of DDE yet recorded for that species. Although both Europe and North America placed restrictions on the use of organochlorines in the late sixties and early seventies, factories in these same countries still produce and market DDT and other known environmentally hazardous pesticides. The market has simply shifted southward. Today, the heaviest use occurs in a broad band across Central America, northern Africa, the Middle East,

Left: Red-shouldered hawk hunting from a tree.

Far Right: Flammulated owl eating a grasshopper.

Near Right: The eastern screech owl, exhibits both a gray and a red phase. The rust-colored plumage of this owl may be an adaptation to further concealment within eastern hardwood forests which have a broader display of colors in the fall.

Left: Peregrine falcon populations have slowly declined throughout the world since the introduction of DDT in 1939. Captive breeding programs in recent years, however, have successfully reintroduced peregrines into many of their original territories.

Right: Birds that feed on other birds, fish, or carnivores will have much higher pesticide levels than birds who feed primarily on herbivorous animals. Because the bald eagle feeds on all three types, it has been more affected by chemical contamination than some raptors.

India, and southeast Asia. Indeed, on a world scale organochlorine use is increasing. As a result, migratory birds bring these toxic chemicals back to the countries where the pesticides were made, in the tissues of their bodies. Nonmigratory raptors are then contaminated when they feed on migratory prey species.

DDT is only one of many toxic chemicals affecting raptors and the health of our environment. Another hazardous group of chemicals is PCBs, industrially produced compounds contained in many paints, resins, plastics, and lubricants. When these products are burned, PCBs enter the environment. Like insecticides, they then accumulate in animal tissues because they are fat soluble. Ultimately, they have the same effect on raptors as DDT, being ingested owing to biological concentration in the food chain and causing population declines through reproductive failure.

Many pesticides, fungicides, and herbicides are used in North American agriculture today. Most of them are designed to decompose and break down quickly; in this respect, these new chemicals are an improvement because they do not concentrate in the food chain. However, they are still exceedingly toxic. Raptors can absorb these chemicals in three ways: in sprayed areas, either directly through their skin or in preening; and by feeding on contaminated prey.

A farmer once called me to say that he'd picked up a sick hawk. When I arrived at his ranch, I found a red-shouldered hawk with symptoms of organophosphate

poisoning: the bird was weak, unable to fly or stand, its eyes were watery, its feet clenched, and its head and neck were shaking. The man said that he had found the bird in the orchard. I then discovered that he had sprayed parathion in the orchard two days earlier. I treated the hawk, but it died two days later.

Two other chemicals identified in recent years as significant threats to wildlife are the heavy metals mercury and lead. Alkyl-mercury, the most common source of mercury contamination on land, has often been used as a seed dressing to protect grain seeds from airborne diseases. Like persistent pesticides, mercury travels from prey to predator and concentrates at the high end of the food chain. The highest levels of mercury among raptor species have been found in falcons and accipiters –

raptors that commonly prey on seed-eating songbirds and rodents.

Lead has long been known to kill waterfowl, which mistake littered lead shotgun pellets for food. Once ingested, as few as one or two pellets can kill birds as large as swans. The U.S. Fish and Wildlife Service estimates that lead poisoning is responsible for the deaths of two to three million waterfowl annually. Lead-poisoned birds often wander away from the flock and retreat into tall grasses or brush, where they are easily captured and consumed by predators, including raptors. In one detailed study of seven hundred bald eagle carcasses, ten percent were found to have died from lead poisoning.

Right: Feathers are connected to muscles which allow a bird to fluff itself out, entrapping the maximum amount of air and enabling the bird to appear larger than normal. Many people assume that birds who are exhibiting this behavior, like the red-shouldered hawk on the right, are fat, when actually they are either trying to keep warm or are displaying defensive behavior to deter predators.

Left: Lead poisoning kills two to three million waterfowl annually. Raptors, like this bald eagle, who feed on poisoned birds ingest the lead pellets contained in their prey, and in turn fall victim to the lead.

ACCIDENTS

Accidents due to human development and expansion also pose significant threats to raptor populations. Roadkill on highways across the United States is estimated by the Humane Society to total over one million animals a day, of which birds account for sixty percent. One study along three hundred and fifty miles of highway in California estimated a roadkill of sixty-one thousand animals monthly.

Many raptors hunt from roadside power poles. These man-made structures provide good perches above the surrounding area, giving the raptors a wide range of vision, easy takeoff, and extra flight speed when attacking prey. Not only do prey along roadsides tend to be visible and vulnerable, but raptors also feed on the many animals killed or injured by passing vehicles. Yet raptors perching on utility poles face a significant threat: electrocution. As consumption of electrical power has increased, many utility poles have become crowded with tightly spaced wires carrying deadly levels of energy. Most birds avoid electrocution by the fact that feathers are very poor conductors of electricity. But if the feathers are wet, or the beak, feet, or skin make contact with the electric wires, birds are usually killed. One Colorado study counted seventeen eagles, one red-tailed hawk, and one great horned owl found dead under three and a half miles of power lines.

Poles can be modified by spacing wires farther apart, placing triangles on top to discourage perching, or increasing wire insulation. For raptors, the best solution is to equip each pole with a special perch that rises above the wire-supporting cross-arms. This last option is of course expensive, but in areas of high raptor use it prevents power outages and enables the birds to utilize the poles safely for hunting.

Although this power pole has not been modified, many utility companies have recently added perches to poles in areas where raptor use is particularly high. This adaption minimizes electrocution and resulting power outages.

Far Right: Already threatened by chemical contamination and habitat loss, raptor populations are very vulnerable to the additional pressures of accidents or — in the case of this golden eagle — illegal shooting.

The Future

As their ancestors have for millions of years, raptors today must overcome many natural factors to survive, including the challenges caused by human expansion. The last fifty years have been hard on raptor populations worldwide as the list of threatened species has steadily grown. We are now sitting at a critical turning point. New knowledge resulting from continued research, coupled with a tremendous increase in public education, has created greater public awareness and concern, as well as the gradual growth of several raptor species.

On June 20, 1782, the U.S. Congress selected the bald eagle to be the national emblem. Unfortunately, this honor did not result in any special treatment. Bald eagle populations continued to decline. Until the National Emblem Law was passed in 1940, bald eagles were shot by the thousands. Golden eagles did not receive protection until 1962. Just when persecution finally slowed, raptors encountered the new threat of chemical contamination. The possibility that the United States might soon be represented by an extinct species helped focus America's attention on the plight of eagles and eventually other raptors as well. DDT was banned, eagle habitat preserves were created, electric

Raptors in North America are now protected by both state and federal laws which make shooting these birds illegal under any circumstances. Unfortunately, some are not deterred by the increased enforcement and penalties, and hunting of raptors, continues.

utility poles were specially modified, and educational efforts further reduced their persecution. In turn, the eagles responded. Today, two hundred years after the bald eagle was selected to be America's symbol, eagle populations are no longer in decline but have begun slowly to increase.

Peregrine falcons also helped to focus research and public attention on raptors. When DDT decimated peregrine populations worldwide, many falconers began to breed their own peregrines. Soon, other raptor species were also successfully bred in captivity, and many large-scale breeding programs were established. In recent years, organizations like the Peregrine Fund have raised and released thousands of birds. Without captive breeding, the peregrine falcon might not have survived the DDT era. Today, however, peregrines once again occupy many territories where they had become extinct.

In light of their positive experience with peregrines, many raptor biologists proposed captive breeding as a means to save the California condor from extinction. Unfortunately, the condor's plight had already become very critical. During the winter of 1984, at which time only sixteen birds were living in captivity, nine of the remaining fifteen wild condors vanished. To ensure genetic diversity and give the condor breeding program a reasonable chance of success, it was decided to trap the remaining wild condors and add them to the captive flock. The decision inspired heated emotions because many believe that when the last free California condor was trapped, on April 19, 1987, condors would become forever extinct as a wild species. Recent events, though, have given

hope that this huge and ancient bird will again fly over North America. Captive breeding has gone well; the condor population has more than doubled from the twenty-two birds of 1985 to fifty-three at the end of the 1991 breeding season. And on January 14, 1992, the Condor Recovery Team released two California condors back into the wild.

Of course, much work still needs to be done to save the California condor, bald eagle, peregrine falcon, and the many other threatened raptors. The ultimate success of captive breeding depends entirely on our ability to preserve an adequate habitat for the birds' use upon release. Although many private, nonprofit organizations worldwide are doing what they can to ensure habitat protection, most depend on public donations.

Left: This bald eagle, found hanging in an illegal pole trap, was emaciated and dehydrated when it was brought to the Raptor Trust, a New Jersey raptor rehabilitation center. Six weeks later, before releasing the bird back into the wild, it is fitted with a band and a radio transmitter to enable tracking.

Top: In order to successfully return captive-bred birds to the wild, like this Harris hawk, a puppet that looks like the young bird's mother is used to feed the bird. Human bodies and hands must be completely hidden to avoid imprinting.

Bottom: Many wildlife rehabilitation centers are now helping to raise orphaned raptors, like these three young great-horned owls.

Where habitat has already been degraded, many people are working to improve marginal habitats by erecting nesting boxes or baskets to replace harvested trees. This effort has resulted in local population increases of several owl species, most notably Ural and boreal owls in Europe. Also accepting nest boxes are barred, saw-whet, screech, barn, little, tawny, and pygmy owls, as well as kestrels, and most likely other cavity-nesting falcons. Ospreys and great gray owls are both known to accept wooden platforms on poles, replacements for dead snags.

Nesting boxes, of course, cannot take the place of quality habitat. In the 1980s, the Raptor Rehabilitation and Propagation Project released nearly five hundred barn owls in Missouri over a six-year period,

and the State Iowa Conservation Department released two hundred and fifty of the birds. Neither project increased owl populations; the release areas no longer offered an adequate supply of food.

The future of raptors depends on the actions of human beings. Will we someday be forced to breed spotted owls in captivity while we try to recreate old-growth forest habitat? Will we preserve enough remaining habitat to ensure the future of threatened raptor populations? Will we convince agriculturalists worldwide to use alternative methods of pest control rather than toxic chemicals? Will we ever end the illegal trapping and shooting of raptors? These are challenging questions, but they must be addressed if raptors are to continue their uphill battle to survive in today's world.

Near Right: *Despite the fact that all raptors are protected by both state and federal laws, illegal hunting of raptors, such as this rough-legged hawk, continues.*

Far Right: *In the absence of education, emotions and misinformation often outweigh research in the heated debate of whether we should limit the continued harvest of old-growth forest habitat.*

Index